Original title:
Lily Pad Lullabies

Copyright © 2025 Creative Arts Management OÜ
All rights reserved.

Author: Victor Mercer
ISBN HARDBACK: 978-1-80566-773-5
ISBN PAPERBACK: 978-1-80566-843-5

Waterside Whispers at Midnight

By the moonlight, frogs do croak,
Wearing hats, they sit and joke.
Tadpoles dance in silly lines,
Chasing bugs in grand designs.

Dragonflies spin tales so tall,
Claiming they can soar and crawl.
A raccoon dons a fancier coat,
Riding on a toad's old boat.

Stars above begin to wink,
While fish below start to think.
A splash! A laugh! The night's a blast,
As belly flops make ripples fast.

All around, the water glows,
Lit by giggles, laughter flows.
Nature's stage where antics bloom,
In a world where frogs consume.

Crickets' Chorus Near the Lagoon

Crickets gather for their show,
Singing loud, in rows they go.
One's off-key, much to delight,
Causing frogs to join the fight.

They play drums on hollow logs,
While nearby lounges a bunch of frogs.
In tuxedos, they sway and spin,
Trying hard to fit right in.

Overhead, a bat takes flight,
Joining in the fun-filled night.
A splash from fish makes crickets jump,
As laughter echoes with a thump.

At the water's edge they prance,
In moonlit beams, they laugh and dance.
With chirps and croaks, a melody grows,
In this lagoon where humor flows.

Swirling Patterns in the Stillness

In a pond where the frogs will gleam,
They dance like ripples in a dream.
With belly flops, they splash and dive,
Each leap a joke that keeps them alive.

When dragonflies crash like silly cars,
The frogs just laugh, my oh my stars!
A chorus of croaks, a ribbit spree,
Nature's laughter, oh so free!

Cradled by Nature's Lullaby

Beneath the moon in silver light,
A sleepy frog hops left, then right.
He sings a tune, sweet and absurd,
To dream of bugs—oh how they chirp!

With sleepy eyes and yawns so grand,
He stretches wide, no one can stand—
The sleepy dance, it takes its toll,
While crickets giggle, all in control!

Ebb and Flow of Dreams

In rippling waters, dreams arise,
A fish swims by, oh what a surprise!
It's the floaters' ball, and they can't be late,
But watch your step—beware the bait!

As they twirl and twist beneath the stars,
The frogs in attendance sing from jars.
A party of splashes, grins, and glee,
Floating through the night, wild and free!

Frogs Sing to the Stars

On lily leaves, the frogs do play,
They reach for stars and sway all day.
Their voices rise in silly cheer,
While crickets join in, loud and clear.

They croak and jump with utmost pride,
Winking at fireflies that glide.
With every leap, the laughter grows,
Underneath the moon, their joy just flows!

The Song of Whispering Willows

Beneath the branches, frogs begin to croak,
They sing of dreams while jesting like a joke.
A mischievous breeze tickles their slimy skin,
As dragonflies dance like they're all wearing tin.

The crickets chirp while the turtles all grin,
One slips and splashes, causing quite the din.
The cattails sway, giggling under the moon,
While owls hoot jokes in a comical tune.

Comfort in the Quietude

In the soft stillness, a bee starts to snort,
Buzzing along like it's played a fine sport.
The puddle reflects a frog's funny face,
As he hops in circles, setting quite the pace.

A turtle chuckles, slow as molasses,
As the fish tell tales, diving with graces.
The reeds shake their heads, making quite the scene,
In this wacky world, serene yet obscene.

Enchanted Evenings by the Waters

Evening descends with a splash and a leap,
Fish whisper secrets, while frogs take a peek.
The moon blinks slyly, giving a wink,
As raccoons waddle home, drunk on the drink.

A silent rabbit jumps with a gleeful shout,
Chasing fireflies, gold dusting about.
The herons in hats strut around the marsh,
Like they're at a party, moving with a lurch.

Soft Serenades in the Marshlands

In the marsh, a melody wafts from the reeds,
A chorus of giggles, sprouting like seeds.
The dragonflies wear tiny tuxedos of light,
Buzzing with laughter as day turns to night.

A raccoon picks berries, its face full of glee,
While witty little frogs plot a new jubilee.
With bulging cheeks, they croon to the stars,
Their harmonies rising like dirty old cars.

The Night's Gentle Cradle

Frogs wear pajamas, snug and tight,
Croaking tales till the morning light.
Crickets giggle, hopping around,
On lily pads, soft sounds abound.

The moon plays tag with clouds so round,
While sleepy fish make barely a sound.
Sleepy turtles snore in delight,
In this sleepy kingdom, all feels right.

Moonlit Reflections Upon the Water

Bubbles rise like giddy dreams,
As goldfish dance in silver beams.
A snail with jazz moves by so slow,
While water lilies sway to and fro.

Waves tickle frogs on their backs,
Filling the night with silly quacks.
Stars wink at the splashing crew,
As friends gather for a night so new.

Sweetness in Still Waters

A sleepy toad gives a great yawn,
As dragonflies tease him until dawn.
Their laughter bubbles, echo through trees,
The breeze joins in with tiny sneezes.

The sleepy pond is quite the show,
With dancing reeds and a soft glow.
Near the shores, a raccoon sneaks,
Laughing at frogs with funny squeaks.

A Symphony of Rest

The night air hums a silly tune,
While shadows stretch beneath the moon.
A raccoon strums on a leafy lyre,
As fireflies spark their fairy choir.

Mice drumbeat softly on the shore,
While turtles join with a sleepy snore.
In this nighttime circus of fun,
All critters rest when the show is done.

The Secrets of the Quiet Swamp

In the stillness, frogs wear hats,
Making plans with chatty bats.
A turtle with a monocle peeks,
While a dragonfly just giggles and squeaks.

The reeds dance to a silent song,
As a fish sings loud, but not for long.
A heron with a bowtie grins,
Counting all his quirky fins.

Dreamscapes in the Moonlight

Bubbles rise from a sleepy bog,
Echoing the snores of a happy frog.
Crickets chirp in silly pairs,
While a snail busks with flair and stares.

Moonbeams tickle the nearest tree,
As a raccoon plays harmony.
Marshmallows float on the river's sway,
Laughing softly at the end of day.

Botanical Nocturne

Plants gossip in the midnight glow,
About a cat that put on a show.
Sunflowers waltz with sleepy vines,
As a lazy hippo does funny signs.

Worms in tuxedos do the twist,
While soil ponders what it missed.
A beetle rolls his tiny drum,
In rhythm to the nighttime hum.

Fables of the Foggy Bay

In the fog, a chicken sails,
On a boat made of giant snail trails.
Pelicans jive in a feathered ball,
While a crab in boots stands proud and tall.

A clever otter makes a rhyme,
Sharing snacks at the perfect time.
Mermaids giggle at a fishy dance,
While seaweed sways in a watery prance.

In the Arms of Gentle Waves

A frog once sang beneath the moon,
His voice was silly, quite a tune.
He ribbited loud, then jumped with glee,
Dance with the fish, come sing with me!

With splashes loud and winks so bright,
They twirled in ripples, what a sight!
The tadpoles giggled, spun around,
While crickets played a bouncy sound.

Nature's Nighttime Sonnet

In the dark, the fireflies blink,
They tease the night, it makes you think.
"Catch me if you can!" they jest,
A game of hide and seek, the best!

The owls hoot jokes, so wise and spry,
"Why did the bat not fly so high?"
For every answer, a chuckle fair,
As nighttime's laughter fills the air.

Petals Swaying in a Soft Breeze

Daisies danced in a playful swirl,
They tickled bees, oh what a whirl!
A shy sunflower peeked and said,
"Why not join us?"—that's how it spread.

With giggles sweet, they spun around,
As petals fell softly to the ground.
The best of friends, they laughed all night,
Under stars that twinkled bright.

Melodies Carried by the Wind

A squirrel strummed on an acorn drum,
With tunes so silly, made us hum.
His tail wagged high, he was the star,
Even the ants came from afar!

The wind joined in with a gentle sigh,
"Let's dance together, oh my, oh my!"
And soon the forest was full of cheer,
With laughter echoing far and near.

Haikus Under the Moon

Frogs croak out their tunes,
While crickets join the choir,
A splash, a leap, a joke,
Nature's midnight fire.

Bubbles burst with glee,
As fish dance in delight,
Laughter fills the pond,
In the soft twilight.

The Lure of Marsh Mornings

Morning mist does twirl,
Like dancers in a show,
A heron takes a bow,
While frogs croak, off we go!

Dragonflies in flight,
Zipping through the dew drops,
Nature's race begins,
No time for sleepy slops.

Calm Currents of Memory

Ripples tell their tales,
Of silly summer dreams,
With giggles in the air,
And sunshine's golden beams.

Toadstools serve as seats,
For stories, laughs, and pranks,
Each splash a punchline,
On memory's riverbanks.

A Dreamer's Harbor

Nighttime brings a jest,
As stars giggle and wink,
The moon tells silly tales,
In a dreamy pink ink.

Where boats made of reeds,
Float on clouds of delight,
Dreamers laugh aloud,
In the soft silver light.

Twinkling Dreams on Water's Edge

Little frogs in tiny hats,
Jump and dance on water mats.
They croak a tune, a silly sound,
As fireflies twirl and spin around.

Wiggly worms bring snacks for all,
Bouncing high, they start to crawl.
Underneath the moon's bright glare,
Frogs in jest fill the night air.

Splashing ripples, laughter flows,
Counting stars as the night glows.
With each leap, a silly cheer,
Making echoes far and near.

Sounds of Serenity at Dusk

Whimsical whispers from the reeds,
As frogs tell tales of nightly deeds.
The crickets chirp a rhythmic beat,
While turtles tap their little feet.

Bubbles rising, frothy glee,
The fish join in for a funny spree.
A splash here, a splash there,
Making waves without a care.

Underneath the painted sky,
A frog jumps up, oh my, oh my!
Laughter echoes in the breeze,
Tickling the grass beneath the trees.

Peaceful Slumber on Verdant Shores

Lazy days on the lush green grass,
Frogs on floats, they gently pass.
Swaying softly, in heat they bask,
While dragonflies play hide and task.

Whispers of wind through leafy trees,
Silly antics, oh what a tease!
A frog falls in with a great big splash,
Landing right in a lily's stash.

Nonsense giggles, soft and sweet,
As sleepy eyes can barely greet.
The moon begins its gentle rise,
While laughter drifts in starry skies.

Echoes of Twilight's Embrace

As the sun dips low, the night ensues,
Frogs in pajamas make their muses.
Chasing shadows with silly hops,
Huddling close, till the laughter stops.

With squeaky voices, they croon and croak,
Bouncing high like a playful joke.
A toad sings loudly, given the chance,
Spreading joy with a clumsy dance.

The moon chuckles, reflecting their fun,
In a moment of glee, the night is won.
Silly stories shared with delight,
Under the sparkling blanket of night.

Dappled Reflections at Dawn

Frogs in tuxedos, a dance on the green,
With wobbly legs, it's quite the scene.
They leap and they flop, with giggles abound,
Their jumps like confetti, splashing all around.

Dragonflies buzzing, with style so grand,
Waving their wings, they join the band.
A chorus of croaks, in melodious cheer,
As dawn brings the laughter, oh, what a year!

The Sound of Soft Ripples

Bubbles rise up from a skimming snail,
Wiggling its way through a slimy trail.
The ducks quack in harmony, quite out of tune,
Splashing like students, once locked in a room.

A turtle named Ted, in his cap and shades,
Suns himself gently, while mischief invades.
His buddy the frog, with a splat and a thud,
Joins in the fun with a terrible thud!

Whimsical Waters

Bouncing pebbles dance in the stream,
As fish play tag—oh, what a dream!
A heron did pirouette, not so composed,
Toppling over, much to the toad's chosed.

The sun sets low, with a wink and a grin,
As creatures gather for the nighttime win.
They share tales of oddities, laughter that swells,
Each story a sprinkle, a swirl of new spells.

Serenities of the Swamp

In a misty swamp, where the giggles collide,
Swans don feather boas—oh, what a ride!
Pigs in a mud bath, lounging in style,
Eying the antics with a cheeky smile.

The ocellaris fish, with their dance so absurd,
Spin circles and twirls, not bothering a bird.
The night hums with laughter, as critters unite,
In a swamp full of joy, all feels just right.

Nocturnal Harmonies of the Wetlands

A frog strummed a tune on a leaf so wide,
While crickets joined in, all hopping with pride.
The night air was thick with their silly songs,
As the moonlight chuckled, 'This won't take long!'

The turtles were swaying, all caught in the groove,
With dragonflies buzzing, they shuffled and moved.
The reeds danced along, in a fashionable sway,
As the frogs took a bow, 'It's hip-hop today!'

Sleepy Shores and Gentle Breezes

On shores where the fireflies twinkled and twirled,
A clam sighed, 'This night's quite the whimsical world!'
Seashells rolled over, trying hard not to snore,
While the sand crabs giggled, 'Give us just one more!'

The wave's gentle laughter tickled the sand,
A hermit crab whispered, 'Is that a song band?'
With whispers and hums, they formed quite a band,
As starfish applauded, the night was so grand!

Toads' Ballet Under the Moonlight

Beneath the bright moon, the toads took the stage,
With twirls and leaps, they danced through the age.
Each hop was a giggle, each spin quite absurd,
With frogs at the front, it was simply unheard!

The crickets, the band, played their fiddles so sweet,
While snails formed a line, moving slow on their feet.
The lily pads quivered with laughter and cheer,
'Join us for fun!' the shadows would jeer!

The Quiet Chorus of the Sedge

In the edge of the sedge, where whispers conspire,
A chorus of critters, with antics so dire.
They croaked and they chirped in a cacophony loud,
While the reeds swayed and nodded, feeling quite proud.

The otters wiggled, in jazz hands and leaps,
While the minnows danced on, in synchronized peeps.
The moon shone down, casting shadows so funny,
As frogs took a selfie, 'We're so slimy and sunny!'

Dappled Shadows and Whispered Wishes

In the pond, frogs dance and leap,
A symphony as crickets peep.
Tadpoles twirl in a water ballet,
While dragonflies giggle, come what may.

Bubbles pop, causing great surprise,
As a minnow flips, oh how it flies!
The moon grins wide, casting its glow,
Tickling the marsh, making it flow.

Lullabies of the Marshlight

The fireflies flash like tiny stars,
Holding dances, strumming guitars.
A sleepy raccoon takes a glance,
At frogs in a very awkward dance.

The reeds sway gently, tell a tale,
Of fish who dreamed to take the rail.
Each splash a giggle from the grass,
As frogs in tuxedos give their sass.

Evening Stillness: Echoes of Nature

The frogs croak out their nightly song,
Like karaoke, they sing along.
A turtle snoozes, basking in pride,
While the pond reflects the moon's wide ride.

A heron prances, a wobbly sight,
In search of lunch under the moonlight.
With a flapping splash, it missed the mark,
And water-danced straight into the dark.

Serenities in the Sunlit Glade

Underneath trees with laughter leaves,
Nature's comic gold, it weaves.
A grasshopper croons, a stand-up star,
While lizards giggle, sitting afar.

Sunbeams tumble on the water's face,
As tiny fish race in a merry chase.
A chorus of chirps and giddy sounds,
In this green kingdom, joy abounds.

A Symphony Beneath the Stars

In moonlit dance, frogs croak a tune,
While fireflies waltz, lighting the gloom.
Crickets join in with a chirpy beat,
A band of nature, so silly and sweet.

A turtle grins, wearing a hat,
Sings to the stars, just imagine that!
The pond reflects giggles, not cries,
As splashes of joy leap up to the skies.

A fish does a jig, quite proud of his show,
While a sneaky old toad steals the glow.
With each little hop and playful sigh,
The night plays along, oh my, oh my!

So gather around, let laughter take flight,
In this wild serenade of the night.
With each croaky note and splashy cheer,
The symphony swells, come join us here!

Reflection and Reverie in Stillness

In the pond's mirror, a duck strikes a pose,
Preening and posing, as everyone knows.
A shy little frog tries to hop in the day,
But slips and tumbles in a most awkward way.

The reeds sway gently, they giggle and sway,
Watching the antics in their own quirky way.
A fish blows bubbles, a smile so wide,
While dragonflies zip like they're on a ride.

In quiet contemplation, a heron waits still,
But a bug flies by, and he nearly gets ill.
With a flap and a splatter, the calm is disturbed,
A splashy ballet that left all perturbed!

As shadows grow long and the sun starts to yawn,
The critters all gather to share tales till dawn.
Each tale a giggle, each laugh a delight,
In the stillness of life, the funny takes flight!

Melodies of the Mellow Marsh

In the soft green bulrush, a chorus begins,
With croaks that resemble some off-key violins.
A turtle, half-spinning, thinks he's on stage,
While the cattails all whisper, 'He's certainly aged!'

The dragonflies zoom in some dizzying arcs,
Chasing their shadows that dance with the larks.
A misunderstood snail tries out his best,
But swiftly retreats, claiming it was a test.

Beneath banded reeds, the silliness flows,
As the fish juggle pebbles with fins and with toes.
The marsh is alive with merriment bold,
A riot of laughter, in stories retold!

As dusk wraps the marsh in a velvety hue,
Even frogs know the fun must be curbed, it's true!
Yet a final croaky note rises with cheer,
In the mellow marsh sound, there's nothing to fear!

Enchanted Evenings by the Riverbank

By the river's embrace, a splurge of delight,
Where shadows and chuckles paint pictures so light.
A raccoon attempts a rather bold stunt,
Stumbling right into a fishy old hunt.

The fireflies laugh as they wink and they blink,
While frogs gather round, all giggling, I think.
A wise old owl hoots some silly old jokes,
The laughter it echoes from the heart of the folks.

With stars overhead in a twinkling spree,
The world looks on, sipping sweet jubilee.
While a duck tells a tale of a runaway shoe,
The river snickers, oh, it's laughing too!

So dance by the foam, let joy take a chance,
Join the frolicsome critters in their nightly dance.
As whispers of humor drift soft on the breeze,
By the riverbank's laughter, we find our hearts ease!

Secrets Beneath the Surface

Bubbles rise with a giggle,
Frogs discuss their best wiggle.
Turtles try to pull a prank,
Splashing guards at the bank!

Fish wear hats, it's a sight!
Swapping tales till it's night.
What's that secret, do you know?
You'll find out if you go slow!

The Solitude of Evening Harmony

Crickets chirp their evening tune,
As they dance beneath the moon.
A raccoon juggles berries bright,
Before it takes its sleepy flight.

The heron's snores echo wide,
While turtles roll for a slide.
A night owl winks with a flair,
As you drift into the air.

Swamp Serenades of the Night

Glowworms hang their tiny lights,
While gators plan their midnight bites.
Mosquitoes hum a buzzing tune,
Often lured by the light of the moon.

A raccoon with a muddy whisk,
Sings a song while taking a risk.
The frogs in chorus croak in glee,
As splashy dancers set them free!

Flickering Fireflies

Fireflies play a game of tag,
With flashes bright, they dance and brag.
One says, "Catch me if you dare!"
While the others float in the air.

Over the reeds they twinkle tight,
Creating magic in the night.
Winking softly, they laugh in flight,
As shadows blend with sheer delight.

Sleeping Dreams

In marshy beds where critters dream,
Snoring softly, a funny theme.
Frogs wear pajamas, all in style,
While fish float by with a cheeky smile.

Crickets keep watch with sleepy eyes,
While whispers float through mossy skies.
Nighttime giggles fill the air,
As sleepy creatures rest with care.

Reflections on a Restful Night

In water's mirror, frogs take flight,
Croaking jokes until it's light.
They wear the crown of slimy green,
With antics only night has seen.

The dragonflies dart, a dizzy show,
Making the lily pads spin and glow.
With splashes and hops, a comic scene,
As crickets chirp, creating a meme.

With each jump, splashes paint the air,
Frogs laugh and tease without a care.
They hold a party till dawn's embrace,
In their own wild, waterlogged space.

Under the Watchful Moon

The moon peeks in, a silver spy,
As frogs compete to leap and fly.
They lose their grace, they trip and fumble,
Creating ripples as they tumble.

A turtle snickers from the shore,
With a slow clap, he begs for more.
With each belly flop, a chorus roars,
Under the moon, laughter soars.

A fish jumps high with gleeful flair,
And lands with a splash—oh, what a pair!
The moon just chuckles, lighting the skies,
In this nightly circus of joyful cries.

A Haven Among the Reeds

In whispers soft, the reeds conspire,
To hide the pranks that frogs require.
They leap and croak with glee all night,
As fireflies join the playful fight.

A raccoon peeks with eyes so wide,
Watching the chaos, but tries to hide.
With sticky paws and playful grace,
He joins the dance, takes his place.

As ripples swirl in moonlit gleam,
The creatures play as if in a dream.
Under the stars, they share their jest,
In this haven where all can rest.

Nighttime Tales of the Water's Edge

Gather 'round, it's story time,
From croaks and chirps, tales will climb.
A frog in slippers slipped on a bug,
Now makes a splash, what a funny tug!

A fish with dreams of flying high,
Practiced jumps that made him sigh.
His leaps were grand, yet oh so bleak,
With belly flops, he'd squeak and squeak.

The cattails sway with laughter near,
As critters tell tales for all to hear.
In moonlit glow, laughter flows,
Nighttime tales, where joy bestows.

Beneath Mossy Canopies

Under the green, the frogs do leap,
They croak and giggle, not lose sleep.
A bird dropped by with a wormy snack,
He tripped on air and fell right back.

Beneath the shade where shadows play,
The critters dance, they laugh all day.
A snail in boots tried to sprint,
But slipped and slid, what a sight to print!

Butterflies with hats take flight,
They chase each other left and right.
But landing softly on a leaf,
They topple down with comic grief.

The sun peeks through with a cheeky grin,
As nature's jokes are set to spin.
Each splash and croak, a silly show,
In their green world, the giggles grow.

Enchanted Waterside Serenade

By the pond where the ripples dance,
A turtle winks, oh what a chance!
He wears a bow tie made of reeds,
And whispers secrets, quick like seeds.

Crickets play their tiny tunes,
Under shimmering silver moons.
A frog in cool sunglasses croaks,
'Your jokes are funny, but mine have strokes!'

The fish below with scales of sheen,
Swim in circles, so serene.
One says, 'Let's dive for a game!'
But belly flops bring them all the fame!

And as the fireflies blink and swirl,
A dancing ant begins to twirl.
With laughter ringing through the night,
The water winks with sheer delight.

Sleepy Tides and Floating Fronds

On floating fronds where laughter lies,
A sleepy duck whispers soft goodbyes.
Her dreams are filled with feathery fun,
While frogs play cards under the sun.

The fish in line tell tall fish tales,
About brave quests and windy gales.
But then they giggle, 'We know what's real!
We once caught grass, now that's a deal!'

The breeze is ticklish on the lake,
As turtles tease and stir awake.
With every splash, a chuckle's shared,
In a sleepy world, all hearts are bared.

So rest your head beneath the trees,
Where honeyed laughs float with the breeze.
Each sleepy wave a funny wink,
On floating fronds, the dreamers think.

The Calm Between Raindrops

In the hush before raindrops play,
The frogs sit still, prepared to sway.
They hum a tune, oh what a sound,
As laughter jumps from round to round.

A ladybug, with dots so bright,
Pretends to be a superhero knight.
With tiny wings and a fearless heart,
She dashes forth to play her part.

The clouds above wear fluffy hats,
While squirrels sing out like acrobats.
They leap from branch to branch with flair,
In that calm moment, laughter fills the air.

And just before the downpour starts,
A frog with dreams leaps into arts.
He paints with rain, a wobbly frame,
In the calm's embrace, we're all the same.

Shadows of the Water Lilies

Bouncing frogs in funny hats,
Dance about like chubby cats.
With a splash and a little skip,
They hold a wild, wobbly trip.

Dragonflies with glittery wings,
Buzz around like tiny kings.
They laugh as they bump and dart,
Creating chaos, playing art.

Turtles giggle on a log,
Waving hello to a passing frog.
With a croak and a cheeky grin,
They cheer for fun, let the games begin.

The moonlight winks upon the waves,
As nighttime urges all to behave.
Yet frogs still jump and shout aloud,
In this green, hilarious crowd.

Night Songs of the Swaying Leaves

Leaves are whispering old, silly tales,
About chubby snails and their tiny trails.
They shimmy and shake in the gentle breeze,
While crickets serenade with playful wheezes.

A squirrel jives on the thick tree limb,
With acorns in tow, he's looking so prim.
He tells the stars to join the fun,
As leaves sway and dance, each a little spun.

Fireflies twinkle, putting on a show,
Making wishes that happily glow.
With flickering laughs, they gleam and tease,
While frogs start to croak in a rhythm with ease.

The shadows play tricks on sleepy heads,
As the night orchestra fills up the spreads.
With giggles, the woods become a stage,
In this funny dance, we all engage!

Echoes in the Pond

A plump little frog took a leap and splat,
Creating echoes that went flat.
His buddy chuckled from the reeds,
Hoping the splash met all his needs.

Ripples giggle, spreading around,
Tickling toads with a funny sound.
They croak in rhythm, a jazz with flair,
As fish swim by without a care.

A duck joins in with a waddling beat,
Singing songs from its fluffy seat.
With quacks and splashes, the fun will thrive,
In their watery world, they come alive.

Under the glow of the distant light,
The pond holds laughter through the night.
Each echo a promise of joy untold,
In this silly pond where stories unfold.

Resting Under the Starry Veil

On a blanket of blooms, frogs recline,
Swapping tales about their next big dine.
With tales of flies that dance and zoom,
They laugh and chuckle in the twilight gloom.

The crickets chuckle, "Let's plan a feast!"
While the fireflies flash to join the beast.
Together they dream of sweet, fly-flavored,
Buffets under stars that shimmer and waver.

The breeze brings whispers of hopes and dreams,
As leaves applaud with their gentle beams.
They dance to the rhythm of giddy delight,
In this party that twinkles deep into the night.

Resting here, as the shadows blend,
Every creature knows, there's no time to end.
With laughter and fun, the world feels right,
Under the starry veil, hearts take flight.

Whispers on Water's Surface

In a pond where frogs do croak,
A turtle cracks a silly joke.
The fish all giggle, swim in circles,
While ducks wear hats and sing in burbles.

A dragonfly zooms, trying to dance,
Stumbling through an awkward prance.
The toads applaud with great delight,
As nighttime falls, it's quite a sight.

Stars twinkle above, as if they know,
This pond is where the fun will flow.
With bubbles rising, laughter loud,
Our water friends form quite a crowd.

So if you pass by, take a peek,
You'll find a party, it's unique!
The bubbles float, the leaves do sway,
In this funny pond, we play all day.

Serenade of the Still Pond

Beneath the moon, the frogs collide,
  With polka dots and silly pride.
They croak a tune that's off-key too,
  Making fish giggle, feeling blue!

A snail slips by, all shiny and slow,
  Whispers of joy as breezes blow.
The reeds sway gently, dance like mad,
While dragonflies mock the ones who're sad.

With fireflies flashing, the stage is set,
  For a midnight concert, no regrets!
The cattails sway, they clap their hands,
  Joining in on this funny band.

In stillness of night, pure laughter glows,
For everyone's welcome, even their toes!
  So join the fun in this joyous spree,
  At the serenade, come sing with me!

Moonlit Reflections in Tranquil Waters

Under the moon, the pond does gleam,
Where fish play tag, it's like a dream.
A frog in shades begins to croon,
With frogs and bugs, a wacky tune.

The heron laughs, with legs so long,
He takes a dip, but it feels wrong.
With a flail and splash, he makes a scene,
Leaves dragonflies giggling in between.

The lily blooms, a dance floor bright,
Where critters gather, a silly sight.
The shadows flicker, tricks abound,
In this night where laughter's found.

So when the moon beams on the scene,
Remember this pond is the place to be seen!
With quips and quacks, the joy won't fade,
In water's embrace, fun's always made.

Floating Dreams Beneath the Stars

On a raft made of leaves, a turtle floats,
With bugs in bow ties and dapper coats.
They toast to the night with acorn cups,
While under the stars, the laughter erupts.

A beaver drifts by with a grin so wide,
Shouting, "Join me in this silly ride!"
The frogs jump ship, they dance in glee,
The turtles twirl in harmony.

A cheeky fish flips, putting on a show,
With every splash, the giggles grow.
The moon winks down, a cheeky spy,
As the ruckus continues, oh me, oh my!

As dreams take flight on soft moonbeams,
This pond at night is bursting at the seams.
So let the frogs sing, let the fish splash,
In this whimsical water, joys are a splash!

Nightfall's Caress on Soft Blooms

As night falls snug on flowers bright,
Frogs sing tunes in pure delight.
Their croaks and chirps mix in the air,
Reed dancers jig without a care.

A bubble pops, a splash of fun,
The party's on, the day is done.
A firefly winks, a prankster's light,
As lily blooms laugh at the night.

Hushed Harmonies of the Pond

In twilight's hush, the critters chat,
A raccoon sneaks by, wearing a hat.
The dragonflies twirl in silly games,
While turtles forget their well-known names.

Soft croaks arise, a froggy band,
With sticks for drums and reeds on hand.
The pond's a stage, with all its charms,
As laughter echoes, and joy disarms.

Petal Whisperings at Twilight

Whispers float on the evening breeze,
As petals giggle atop the trees.
A snail takes a stroll with a wink and a grin,
Saying, 'Slow and steady always wins!'

Bubbles rise from below the sheen,
As fish tell tales about their cuisine.
The water's a canvas, laughter's the paint,
Where frogs make jokes and lilies faint.

Serenade of the Still Waters

Beneath the stars, the water glows,
With quirks and quips, the laughter flows.
A buoyant frog takes center stage,
Reciting puns like a famous sage.

The band of night creatures gather near,
With pop songs that only they can hear.
As ripples dance in moon's soft grace,
They sing their songs, fun smiles on each face.

Pondside Poetics: A Nocturne

At dusk the bugs wear tiny hats,
And dance around like tipsy chaps.
While frogs debate the best of flies,
They croak their tunes beneath starry skies.

The lilies wink with secret glee,
As tadpoles race in a bumblebee.
A heron sneezes, the world stands still,
While crickets chirp, 'What a thrill!'

A turtle sings with shaky flair,
His shell a chair for evening air.
The moonlight plays on lily's sway,
Job offers for bugs come out to play.

In every ripple, laughter's found,
In this pond so merry and round.
Each night's a party, don't be late,
Nature's own hilarious fate.

Soft Echoes from a Moonlit Bay

A raccoon juggles shiny jars,
While frogs recite their finest bars.
The water shimmers with a giggle,
As fireflies dance and make us wiggle.

An otter slips, creates a splash,
Then grins and swims away in a flash.
Barn owls hoot their joyful tune,
While turtles bob, a funny swoon.

Bubbles rise with whispers bold,
From fish with tales of treasures untold.
The night air fills with joyful banter,
While crickets hold a wild canter.

As night deepens, laughter flows,
In the bay where the moonlight glows.
Each wave a chuckle, each breeze a cheer,
Nature's humor shining clear.

Celestial Serenades in Ferny Glades

Beneath the ferns, the stories spin,
As ladybugs wear their silly grins.
A fox, with flair, recites a rhyme,
While owls hoot out the punchline.

The crickets hum a wobbly tune,
While skunks caper 'neath the moon.
With every rustle, laughter's near,
The glade's alive, let's all draw near!

Toads sport ties made of twine,
While beetles debate over the best wine.
A hedgehog winks, 'This party's grand!'
And all the critters clap their hands.

As shadows stretch and giggles bloom,
In the heart of nature, there's always room.
For jest and jive, and joy in spades,
In these ferny nooks, where fun cascades.

Crickets' Choir and Frogs' Fables

In twilight's grasp, the crickets sing,
As frogs exchange their wildest fling.
Each note a splash, each croak a cheer,
This night is filled with chuckles near.

A bassoon frog leads the merry crew,
While dragonflies join, a lively few.
The jokes they weave are quite absurd,
With punchlines snappy, every word!

Beneath the stars, a tale unfolds,
Of friendly toads in coats of gold.
They hop with glee, proudly display,
Their fables spun in froggy play.

As whispers dance across the pond,
All creatures listen, and respond.
In this night, where laughter raves,
A symphony of chirps and waves.

Night Songs of the Marshland

In the dim of the swamp, frogs croon a tune,
Their serenades float under the light of the moon.
Crickets chirp laughs, a delightful brigade,
As bugs dance around, their dinner parade.

Fireflies blink like stars in a jar,
While turtles glide slow, thinking they're a car.
A raccoon with a hat, peeking from a tree,
Says, "Join the feast, come merry with me!"

Splashing and giggling, it's quite a sight,
As the shadows play tag in the fading light.
The marshland invites with a wink and a grin,
For every odd critter to join in the din.

So gather your giggles, we'll dance till we drop,
With raucous cheers echoing, we'll never stop.
In the heart of the marsh, where the echo takes flight,
We'll sing out our laughter and frolic all night.

Gentle Ripples and Soft Suppers

A platypus chef stirs a pot with a smile,
"Join me for dinner, it'll take just a while!"
He flings in some lily, a splash without care,
While ducks draft the menu with flair and a dare.

The turtles are chatting 'bout new dishes to share,
While fish gossip nearby, saying, "Isn't it rare?"
With a croak and a chuckle, the bullfrog does boast,
"Tonight we'll feast on the finest of toast!"

The reeds sway in rhythm, like guests at the dance,
A snail in a tux gets a twirl for romance.
With laughter and stories, the evening goes round,
In a banquet of joy where friendship is found.

So bring out the snacks, let the fun spin around,
In nature's great kitchen, love issues abound.
With flavors of whimsy and giggles to dine,
We'll relish the moments, both silly and fine.

Floating Cradles of Serenity

Upon the calm water, a boat made of leaves,
Drifts softly along, where the dragonfly weaves.
With lilting tunes sung by the breeze as it flows,
Each ripple a secret the marshland bestows.

A sleepwalking otter is dreaming of fish,
While frogs in pajamas make quite the dish.
With winks and with whispers, they tell tales of yore,
Upon floating cradles, they giggle and snore.

As shadows grow longer, the fun never fades,
In the realm of soft crooning where joy serenades.
Each creature a brother, each moment a glee,
In boats made of lily, they float merrily.

The marsh sends a shiver, a tickle and tease,
While the twilight wraps all in a whisper of ease.
Within dewdrop dreams, mischief takes flight,
In floating cradles of silly delight.

The Dance of Arias on Aquatic Stages

On a stage made of water, the singers convene,
Frog tenors and basses, with voices so keen.
They croak under stars, a humorous fuss,
While bumblebees applaud, raising a buzz.

A snail in a bowtie conducts with great flair,
As catfish tap dance, a show beyond compare.
The ladybugs twirl under soft, twinkling lights,
Creating a spectacle that sparkles the nights.

With a hop and a skip, there's laughter galore,
As raccoons throw confetti and shout for encore.
Each splash of a paddle, a rhythm divine,
Celebrating the stage, in a marshland so fine.

So join in the chorus, don't miss the big show,
Where each little creature adds flair to the flow.
A night full of giggles and claps from the crowd,
In watery wonders, let's cheer and be loud!

Tranquil Reflections

Frogs croak serenades, loud and clear,
While bugs dance close, without any fear.
Ripples of laughter across the pond,
Make the still water a stage to respond.

A dragonfly winks, sharp as can be,
Chasing its shadow, just trying to see.
The moon takes a bow, sparkling up high,
As critters below all wish to comply.

Snakes slide with grace, in tuxedos of green,
While turtles, in shorts, put on quite the scene.
The night hums a tune, silly and bright,
Making each moment a joyful delight.

So join in the fun, without any dread,
Where antics abound, and laughter is spread.
For every small splash, and buzzing that sways,
Frogs croon their songs in humorous arrays.

Echoes of the Evening Breeze

The whispering leaves, secrets they share,
With crickets who chirp without any care.
A raccoon performs, on a low-hanging limb,
As shadows dance wildly, their edges all dim.

Fireflies twinkle like stars at play,
While frogs hold a concert, a jazzy soiree.
With hats made of reeds, they strut and they sway,
Making even the night feel like a cabaret.

A mischievous breeze tousles the hair,
Giggling with glee, makes all critters stare.
The pond is a stage for all creatures near,
In a ballet of laughter, it's clear what we hear.

So come join the fun and let worries cease,
In the evening's embrace, we find our peace.
With echoes of joy that bounce through the night,
We dance with the critters, oh what a sight!

Water's Embrace at Dusk

As dusk paints the sky with a cheeky grin,
The pond bubbles over, let the games begin.
Frog divas in gowns croak operatic notes,
While fish in tuxedos jump up on their boats.

A paddleboat turtle plays DJ tonight,
Spinning all beats from left to the right.
With each little splash, and every loud cheer,
The laughter grows louder, it's music we hear.

The lily leaves shimmer, like dance floors of gold,
And each little splash is a story retold.
With giggling minnows, and dapper old frogs,
A gathering of joy, like mind-bending logs.

So paddle on over, join the fun parade,
Where water's our stage, and no debts are paid.
In the laughter of dusk, we find our sweet place,
In nature's embrace, we dance with pure grace.

Silken Slumbers in the Garden

In gardens of dream, where oddities bloom,
Ladybugs wear hats, brightening the gloom.
A sleepy-eyed snail takes a leisurely ride,
While nightshade giggles, saying, "Come, take a slide!"

A caterpillar snores in a bed made of leaves,
While bumblebees buzz with their fanciful eves.
Fireflies flash, like tiny sweet lights,
As crickets compose their nocturnal delights.

The moon joins the party, with a quirky face,
Promising games in the soft moonlit space.
Where laughter is woven through night's calming quilt,
And all of our worries are beautifully built.

So snuggle in tight, let the night carry on,
With whispers and chuckles till the break of the dawn.
For sleep in the garden, oh what a delight,
Where dreams come alive under stars shining bright.

Twilight Melodies of the Quiet Stream

The frogs croak tunes in the fading light,
As dragonflies dance in their funny flight.
Wet leaves giggle with a tickling breeze,
While fish splash joyfully, shaking the trees.

A snail sings softly, creeping on shells,
Telling tales woven with muddy smells.
The water winks back, a cheeky delight,
As stars start to twinkle, giving a fright.

Notes from the Heart of the Waterway.

A turtle wears glasses, looking so wise,
He tells silly jokes, oh how time flies!
The minnows all chuckle, they can't get enough,
While the catfish join in, all giggles and guff.

Beneath the cool lily, an otter does slide,
With a splash and a grin, he takes it in stride.
The reeds sway and sway, joining in the fun,
As the sun sets low, their laughter's begun.

Whispers on the Water

A wise old frog croaks tales of great charms,
As butterflies flirt, with their colorful arms.
The pond is a stage, where all critters play,
And the moon shines a spotlight, lighting their way.

Goldfish wear crowns and swim in a line,
Waving at ducks who think they're divine.
The splashes and laughter create quite the scene,
In the cool evening air, it's a jovial dream.

Gentle Ripples of Night

The night critters gather for a light-hearted spree,
With crickets as DJs, playing songs for free.
Fireflies glow bright, like disco balls,
As frogs croak the chorus; everyone calls!

The moon roars with laughter, tickled pink in the sky,
As turtles tap dance, not caring to shy.
With a ripple of giggles, the night carries on,
In a playful parade till the brightening dawn.

Musings of a Midnight Pond

Frogs all gather for a jam,
With croaks and ribbits, who's the fam?
A toad hops on, a belly flop,
The night so bright, the fun won't stop.

The dragonflies buzz, wearing bling,
They dance like stars on paper wings.
"Oh dear," one says, "I've lost my shoe!"
"Just borrow mine!" a friend will do.

Ripples shimmer, laughter flies,
As herons pretend to exercise.
"Watch my moves!" a frog declares,
But slips and lands—no one else cares.

So sing, dear pond, your songs so sweet,
With goofy beats and flippered feet.
For in this verse, all problems fade,
In the moonlight, joy is made.

Graceful Shadows Cast by the Moon

Under moonbeams, shadows creep,
With giggling tides that never sleep.
Marshland pals in a game of tag,
While a crab sports a tiny rag!

Old turtle slips, says, "Oops, not me!"
As ducks quack loud, they shout with glee.
"Can we all sway like the reeds?" they cheer,
But one flips over, laughs without fear.

The sleepy breeze brings tales from far,
Of slimy slugs on a grapevine car.
Raccoons with snacks make quite a sight,
Popping popcorn under starlight.

So raise a toast with night's laughter,
To shadow dances and silly banter.
For every whisper in the gloom,
Is just a friend with heart to bloom.

The Dreaming Water Nymph

A nymph so sly with a playful grin,
Dances in circles, twirling skin.
With cheeks aglow, and hair so wet,
She dips and dives, no need to fret.

"Oh, look!" she calls to her merry crew,
"Catch me if you can, I'm almost through!"
But frogs just laugh, and splash around,
While fish are giggling without a sound.

A snail keeps pace, with style and flair,
While dragonflies zoom—can they compare?
"Let's have a race!" the nymph shouts loud,
Then trips on reeds, falling with proud.

Bubbles bubbling in a fizzy spree,
All join in, they're silly and free.
Through laughter's stream, dreams take flight,
As night drapes softly, wrapping tight.

Bedtime Stories of the Garden

In the garden where veggies talk,
Tomatoes joke with wise old squash.
"Tell us tales of the night parade,"
"Mice on scooters, our fun is made!"

A chorus of lilies lift their heads,
As radishes spin in their beds.
"Did you see how the owls all danced?"
"Or how that sad worm felt entranced?"

Under the stars, ants form a line,
With witty jokes, they sip on wine.
A caterpillar in a vest so fine,
Has dreams of flying, oh, how divine!

So close your eyes, drift into dreams,
With garden laughter and moonlit beams.
For every story you hear tonight,
Brings joy and giggles until first light.

Watercolor Dreams at Dusk

In twilight's hue, the frogs do croak,
They sing a tune, it's quite a joke.
A dragonfly slips, a belly flop,
And giggles ripple till the night's a-top.

With paints of dreams and laughter bright,
The reeds sway gently, what a sight!
A canvas clear, where giggles blend,
Nature's sketches, joy won't end.

As fireflies dance, they lose their way,
Stumbling on notes of their ballet.
They twirl and dive, oh what a thrill,
In a world where joy waits still.

So gather 'round this silly space,
Where every splash brings a cheerful face.
With watercolor skies, we hang and hum,
In silly dreams, we're never numb.

A Soothing Song for the Still Waters

On quiet shores, a splat and a squee,
The fish chuckle, how funny is he?
Bubbles rise with a wink and a cheer,
As they whisper tales we strain to hear.

The moon peeks down, with a giggly grin,
As turtles race, oh, let the fun begin!
Splashing about, they wiggle and sway,
In watery worlds where they play all day.

A croaking choir begins to compete,
With silly tunes that bounce and repeat.
Their silly songs take wing and fly,
Over the pond where laughter is nigh.

So join the splash, don't be a bore,
With each little leap, let your spirit soar.
In soothing songs, find joy's sweet thrill,
With every giggle, our hearts we fill.

Beneath the Surface: Tales of Tranquility

Under the water, where giggles bloom,
Fishes dance under lily's gloom.
With a flick of a tail, they leap with glee,
In a bubble bath, they have a spree.

Their tales of splashes, from dusk till dawn,
Are filled with laughter, not a yawn.
In watery depths, surprises creep,
Like mischievous crabs that never sleep.

A turtle hums, a beat so sly,
Confusing all that swim nearby.
His serenade drifts, a funny tune,
As bubbles pop under a shining moon.

Oh, come and listen to secrets shared,
In the shimmering waves, joy is declared.
With every splash, a story spins,
Where laughter lingers and adventure begins.

Refuge of the Reeds: Soothing Rhymes

Among the reeds, the crickets chirp,
With rhymes that dance and tickle and burp.
A frog on a log, in his silly hat,
Tells jokes so funny, the fish go splat!

With every twist, the waters giggle,
And ripples form as they start to wiggle.
A heron pauses, looks around,
Wondering who makes that funny sound.

In this leafy refuge, secrets bloom,
Where whimsy wafts and laughter zooms.
A quirky world, beneath the trees,
Where funny tales ride on the breeze.

So curl your toes, enjoy the show,
With every leap, let your laughter flow.
Here in the reeds, serenity gleams,
With soothing rhymes and watercolor dreams.

www.ingramcontent.com/pod-product-compliance
Lightning Source LLC
Chambersburg PA
CBHW051644160426
43209CB00004B/781